blistered asphalt on dixie highway: Kentucky Basketball is Poetry in Motion

poems by

Ron Whitehead

Finishing Line Press
Georgetown, Kentucky

blistered asphalt on dixie highway: Kentucky Basketball is Poetry in Motion

*for my brother, Brad Whitehead,
and the thousands and thousands
of basketball games we played*

Copyright © 2016 by Ron Whitehead
ISBN 978-1-63534-087-7 First Edition
All rights reserved under International and Pan-American Copyright Conventions. No part of this book may be reproduced in any manner whatsoever without written permission from the publisher, except in the case of brief quotations embodied in critical articles and reviews.

ACKNOWLEDGMENTS

Thank you to my longtime friend New York Mets poet Frank Messina for suggesting I write this book and thank you to Nancy Wilson and Jinn Bug for suggesting I submit this book manuscript to the Finishing Line Press competition and thank you Finishing Line Press for the award and a Special thank you to my sweetheart Jinn Bug who has shown me more love and support than I've ever known and without whom this book, and so many other new writings, would have never happened.

Publisher: Leah Maines

Editor: Christen Kincaid

Cover Art: Howard Wilson

Author Photo: Jinn Bug

Cover Design: Elizabeth Maines

Printed in the USA on acid-free paper.
Order online: www.finishinglinepress.com
also available on amazon.com

Author inquiries and mail orders:
Finishing Line Press
P. O. Box 1626
Georgetown, Kentucky 40324
U. S. A.

Table of Contents

blistered asphalt on dixie highway 1
in snow in rain in cold in gloom in kentucky we deliver 2
ping pong living room street ball 3
10 foot shots on an 8 foot goal 5
grade school classroom layup 6
what daddy told the principal 7
kendall "mousie" render was a basketball wizard 8
when the beaver dam beavers went to state 9
shin splints for a centertown demon 11
the death of small town usa 12
getting cut 14
popcorn adolf rupp larry conley tom jones and my brother brad 16
cotton nash and adolf rupp 18
rupp's runts 19
butch beard and wes unseld 20
sweet sixteen runner up 21
breaking and entering basketball 23
gary "lefty" raymond passed the ball to himself 24
nose to nose with john danks oldham park beaver dam basketball 26
i'll break your leg 27
when kenny davis elbowed me i saw stars 29
not without a fight 30
104 degrees in the shade of a saguaro cactus 32
oxford ball 33
elbow at the y 34
sucker punched at freedom hall basketball 35
from kentucky to alphabet city 37
Watching the NBA playoffs with Hunter S. Thompson 38
the comeback kid 39

blistered asphalt on dixie highway

august 1966 i'm 15 we're running full court
shirts and skins blistered asphalt on dixie highway
valley station louisville south end
high top converse black and white
so damn hot the court is sizzling
and so are we pass pass pass
then shoot don't let the ball touch
the street 2 hours running non-stop
loser sits but we keep winning
then cannonball off the high dive
valley swimming pool oh the lovely ladies
crank up WAKY 790 rock n roll radio
blistered asphalt on dixie highway
valley station louisville south end

in snow in rain in cold in gloom in kentucky we deliver

with tape measure and hand saw and hammer and nails
my brother and i built the 2 by 8 oak wood slatted backboard
we added a rim and threaded the net
nailed each side to tall cedar posts
between farmhouse and barn on the south side of the yard
next to our garden and orchard we dug 2 deep holes
soon as daddy got home from the mines he helped us hoist
our new basketball goal into the ground and tamp it down
i got up during the night to watch giant snowflakes fall
but at dawn the flakes lightened and the temperature rose
school was cancelled so after breakfast
we swept the court and as we took our first shots
snow turned to rain the court turned to mud but
my brother and i played and played all day we played
in snow in rain in cold in gloom in kentucky we deliver

ping pong living room street ball

winter lives next door down
the street from fall and

on this 2nd day of fall i'm
thinking about deep winter

blizzard below zero way too
cold to go outside no school today

brad and i were boys playing
ping pong living room street ball

move the furniture to the sides of
the living room and the court is

ready yep we learned a long time
ago how to improvise so we're

using a ping pong ball as our
basketball and the goal well

at the top of the window there's
a 3 inch space between the

curtain rod and the wood
window frame so brad and i are

playing one on one to score you
gotta get the ping pong ball to

go between curtain rod and
window frame and yes after one

game we're experts drilling shots from
inside and from downtown but we're also

making a whole lotta noise plus we're
occasionally damaging furniture so

after a couple of hours mama says
boys why don't you get dressed real

warm and go down to the barn to
play so we get dressed and grab

our real basketball and a piece of
chalk and it's a relief to find that

there's no wind blowing in the
barn well except for what comes through

the cracks but all we care about is
playing ball so i climb the old

wood slat ladder and draw chalk
marks a foot apart on the 2 by 8

oak beam 10 feet up in the entry way the
ball has to land between the chalk marks to

count as a basket and after one
game we're experts so

for the next 2 hours brad and i are
hard at it playing one on one chalk mark

on oak barn ball right after 2 hours of
ping pong living room street ball

10 foot shots on an 8 foot goal

backyard full court
8 foot goal on one end
10 foot on the other
grass worn down to hard dirt

10 foot rim leans to the left
and is too high in the front
8 foot rim sags in front
and leans to the right

it's time to order new nets
from the sears catalog
and we keep pumping air
into the bald basketball

but all we care about is the game
5 on 5 shirts and skins
24 by 2 points and 4 up to win
winning team stays in

keeps playing till the last glimmer
of sunlight is gone
backyard full court
10 foot shots on an 8 foot goal

grade school classroom layup

with 10 seconds to go
at the top of the circle
which was near midcourt

small kentucky
hardwood floor school gym

i faked to the right
then cut to the left
going by my man
down the center of the lane
but as i went up for the open layup
i was pushed hard from behind
propelling me through the door
under the goal into the classroom
where we had put on our uniforms

after tackling 3 wooden desks
i brushed off my bruises and hustled
to the foul line where i hit both free throws

we won the game 12 to 10
grade school classroom layup

what daddy told the principal

daddy was a 10th degree badass a 10th degree smartass
nobody and i mean nobody messed with daddy

daddy was the go to guy he was the godfather
he was a family man a bare knuckle boxer an athlete

a coach a coal miner a farmer
daddy was an all-round great guy but

i'm not sure beaver dam's principal felt the same way
well at least not the night my daddy's brother

my uncle j.r. whitehead's horse branch bears
high school basketball team was playing

the villainous mossie martin's beaver dam
beavers basketball team at the beaver dam gym

daddy and his brother my uncle tony were
yelling real loud at the refs who were making

terrible calls in favor of the home team beaver dam
so the principal came over and said if you don't

quieten down i'm gonna have you removed from
the gym well daddy real mean like leaned in

toward mr. principal and said listen to me you
son of a bitch you're not man enough to throw

me out of this gym or anywhere else so you best
turn around and walk away while you can and

well mr. principal turned white as a ghost drew
a blank look on his bewildered face then turned

and walked away nobody and i mean nobody
messed with daddy and for that matter nobody

and i mean nobody messed with
his brothers my uncles tony and j.r. whitehead

kendall "mousie" render was a basketball wizard

mr. jones stood in the back of his store which
was next door to granddaddy's barber shop in centertown

and watched as my uncle kendall slipped behind the counter
and stole candy but mr. jones didn't mind he thought

it was sweet he told kendall's parents mamaw and
granddaddy but he asked that neither of them tell

kendall cause well he said he liked kendall and
he enjoyed his silent visits kendall was a quiet boy

few knew then how smart he was but many suspected
granddaddy loved basketball so much

he closed his main street barber shop and
went to the gym every time the centertown demons

played at home whenever the boys had an away
game all the men congregated at granddaddy's

barber shop and leaned toward the old radio
to listen as granddaddy's 1st born son

kendall "mousie" render and his best friend
jackie maddox two of the best guards to ever

grace the centertown gym performed such miracles
that some folks called them the diamond duo

everybody called kendall "mousie" cause
well he wasn't that big but was he ever fast

time and again he quicksilver slipped around
his man and drove to the basket for an open layup

he stole the ball like a mouse steals cheese
he earned the school record for steals many folks

said that if the renders hadn't moved to valley station
in south louisville cause raymond "dick" render got

a job as grader operator building the watterson expressway
if they'd just stayed in centertown folks said

no telling what could have happened cause
kendall "mousie" render was a basketball wizard

when the beaver dam beavers went to state

my aunt jo carolyn told the scariest ghost stories
when the beaver dam beavers went to state

we listened to the games on the AM radio
in my aunt jo carolyn's kitchen in the little

stone house she and paul and brucie
lived in below the hill across from

the centertown baptist church graveyard
near sweet olivia doyle's home

our rockport cousins gerald and donnie hoskins
played for beaver dam they were coached

by ohio county legend w.m. "mossie" martin
they won their 1st round game against

glasgow handily 79 to 61 but the quarter final
was a barn burner they played the all black

lexington dunbar team it was neck and neck
all the way but dunbar pulled away at the end

and won 83 to 74 larry conley's ashland team
beat dunbar in the championship game

we stood around my aunt jo carolyn's
kitchen table yelling for beaver dam to win

and we were sorely disappointed when
they lost but that night after the game

my aunt jo carolyn said why don't we walk
up to the graveyard and i'll tell you all

some true ghost stories uh oh soon as
she said those words the hair stood up

on the back of my neck cause i'd been
there before and i knew her stories were

all true so later that night we huddled
down right on top of a grave my aunt jo carolyn

leaned her back up against the tombstone
and as the clouds drifted over the full moon

as the wind started whipping recklessly
my aunt jo carolyn told us a story of the father

who stood in the front yard departing for a
long journey and immediately after he hugged

his wife and children they stood open
mouthed as he vanished right before their

eyes and every year if you go back to that
house which is just below centertown on

the matanzas road if you stand in the front
yard on this particular night the same night

we were sitting on the grave in the centertown
baptist church graveyard when there's a full

moon and the moon was full well you could
hear that man yelling for his family and you

could hear his family screaming for him and
when my aunt jo carolyn got to that part in

the story she screamed so loud her scream
caught my blood on fire and every hair on

my head stood straight up and suddenly
all us kids were on our feet screaming and

running as fast as we could back to
my aunt jo carolyn's house oh my oh my

the year was 1961 i was 10 years old
when the beaver dam beavers went to state

shin splints for a centertown demon

too much too fast too soon
no i'm not talking about bad sex

i'm talking about how i've lived
most of my life till now and i'm

still an ancient child but at age 65
i've started wrapping my mind and actions

round not too much not too fast not too soon
but on a sunny october 1964 afternoon

i was running suicide sprints a member of
the centertown demons' freshman basketball team

wearing black converse no support high tops we
left the gym and took back streets to

main street we ran 3 miles and i
always wanted to be first at anything

and everything well i got out front
and stayed there so the next morning 5am

when my wind-up attic alarm clock went off i
was sure that both my legs were broken

1st time i ever had shin splints but i
was raised to be tough so i never told one soul

cause i was proud to play for the centertown demons
we had a good freshman team fonzo decker and me at

guard doug cavender and jackie tomlinson at
forward and roger catfish givens at center

randy swann was a darn good coach and person
he helped us believe in ourselves

and i'll tell you one thing i'd rather have
shin splints playing basketball than be

riding our horses pulling our wagon through
the bottoms harvesting corn by hand

and well yes for years and years i lived i breathed
too much too fast too soon

and it's not that i'm slowing down i'm simply
having new adventures unraveling new runes

the death of small town usa

remove the school and kill the town
i love small towns and i sure do miss them

in 1963 we had the worst coach
in the history of basketball coaches

but outside school my brother brad and i
were blessed with the best coaches

in the history of coaches yes
i'm talking about daddy and his brother uncle roy

so on the court brad and i coached ourselves
we grew up playing old school ball

run run run pick and roll pass shoot
follow your shot rebound and when

they have the ball get down low stay on
your feet don't go for the fake and

play hardnosed blue collar no blood no foul
working man in your face full court basketball

i brought the ball to the top of the key
brad cut down the side then ran his man

into a baseline pick then i wrist flicked a fast
no look pass to him and brad drilled it from the corner

the hometown standing room only crowd went wild
i was in the 8th grade brad was in the 6th

we were guards for the centertown demons
at every home and away game we played

every small town gym was packed
rockport mchenry beaver dam cromwell horse branch

hartford dundee fordsville pleasant ridge centertown
local schools were the heart and soul of small town usa

centertown school had 300 students grades 1 through 12
after my 9th grade year all the local high schools

consolidated into ohio county high between
hartford and beaver dam over 1,200 students

there were more in my 1968 graduating class than
all students grades 1 through 12 at centertown

remove the school and kill the town
i love small towns and i sure do miss them

some folks say president clinton ended the working class
by signing nafta the north american free trade agreement

some folks say president reagan ended the working class
by firing the air traffic controllers and refusing to hire them back

some folks say sam walton's wal-mart ended the working class
by running all the ma and pa stores out of business

and well i agree with all 3 but i look back and vividly recall
how the consolidation of high schools was the beginning of

the death of small town usa

remove the school and kill the town
i love small towns and i sure do miss them

getting cut

far back as i recall i've been
the leader the captain i've been

in charge of whatever's going on i've always
wanted and expected it to be that way

any other way felt wrong but
has it always been that way well

of course it hasn't the reality is i've been
on the other side of winning so many times

i became a contemplative i journeyed inward
i've spent as much if not more time searching

on the inside as i've spent adventuring
on the outside for example my sophomore

year of high school well i was still
5 feet 4 inches tall when ohio county's

high schools consolidated into one giant
1,200 student school and there i was 13

years old heading into puberty stepping into
many unknown worlds simultaneously and

while studying calculus and trigonometry my
algebra 2 teacher humiliated me in front of

the class by asking me to explain how i derived
my answer which i couldn't do up till then whenever

i saw a question i saw the answer so i turned
away from my teacher and bout the same time

that happened i was the last man cut from
the basketball team i'd always been starting

guard and forever being the youngest in all
my classes having started 1st grade at 5 cause

i loved school and wanted to go and being the
youngest of all my friends them all well into

puberty i was wondering if i'd ever get there yes
i was counting hairs every one of them and i was

praying dear god please help me grow then
puberty finally arrived and it was a nightmare

and once our schools consolidated i hated
school i went underground i became a pirate outlaw

i hid my thoughts and feelings no one understood me
and i kept telling myself i didn't want to be and

i would never be understood i would forever travel
alone and it took me years and years of hard

traveling to heal so many deep and bloody wounds
but i'm stubborn and underneath all my anger rage and

pain i wanted to be whole i wanted to be loved i
wanted to love so i kept on keeping on finding

ragged rugged broken paths to healing i
finally got sick and tired of

getting cut

popcorn adolf rupp larry conley tom jones and my brother brad

some folks become athletes
my brother brad was born an athlete

2 years and 12 days after the kentucky
thanksgiving when i came along

on december 5th 1952
my brother brad was born

there's a photo somewhere of 2 year old brad
in speedo style briefs lifting weights

in baseball brad was catcher and center fielder
in football he was running back
in basketball he played guard

brad played center field like willie mays
brad danced like tom jones
brad was built like hercules

and brad loved popcorn
he was a popcorn fanatic

in 1967 brad and i attended the kentucky
sweet sixteen state high school basketball

tournament at freedom hall the same year
big jim mcdaniels from allen county-scottsville played

the same year lightning fast caneyville from grayson county
made it to the semi-finals

we were on the floor near the court when
brad said i've got to have some popcorn

so we headed to the nearest concession stand
and bought coca colas and boxes of popcorn

then headed quickly back to our seats
well lo and behold as we flew around a corner

we had to put on our brakes to keep from
running smack dab into adolf rupp and

larry conley adolf handed conley two 20 dollar bills
and larry walked away then as in the

blinking of an eye brad ripped the top
off his box of popcorn pulled out a pencil

which i didn't know he had then stepped
up and said mr. rupp my name's brad

may i have your autograph and well
coach rupp stared at brad then grumbled

i reckon so and you know my brother brad
now has that rupp signed popcorn box top framed

and displayed in his living room right over
the chair where he sits and eats popcorn while watching

uk wildcat basketball on tv
popcorn adolf rupp larry conley tom jones and my brother brad

cotton nash and adolf rupp

december 28, 1963 freedom hall louisville kentucky
university of kentucky versus notre dame
my brother brad and i sat behind the baseline bench
we shook hands with cotton nash and adolf rupp
during timeouts we heard rupp chewing
the players out with 17,000 fans we cheered
uk on to a 101 to 81 victory
larry conley 9 points randy embry 10
terry mobley 18 points ted deeken 27
and the hero cotton nash with 33

as kentucky farm boys then teenagers
brad and i were blessed to meet and
receive phone calls from and have dinner
with several governors plus and oh my
the big plus was a few times each year having
the best seats
at university of kentucky and university of louisville
football and basketball games and
cincinnati reds baseball games
brad and i love sports
always have always will

rupp's runts

the man in the brown suit
baron of the bluegrass
4 national championships but

coming off his worst season
expectations were running low
for this new squad lordy the 2nd team

nearly beat them in the final scrimmage
before the season opened the 1960s
weren't looking too good for coach rupp

who now had a litter of runts but don't
ever underestimate a great coach

my brother brad and i sat behind
the bench on the baseline freedom hall
louisville kentucky december 29th 1965
as uk clobbered notre dame 103 to 69

#30 tommy kron scored 7 points
#40 larry conley 13 #55 thad jaracz 16
#10 louie dampier 26 #42 pat riley 36

and surprising everyone
in the ncaa championship game
college park maryland march 19th 1966

uk fell to texas western 72 to 65
ending their season 27 and 2

no matter what anyone says
adolf rupp's 1965-66 team
turned out to be one of
the greatest teams ever

rupp's runts became basketball kings

butch beard and wes unseld

i'm searching for a courier-journal photo
of my brother brad and me playing basketball
spring 1967 freedom hall louisville kentucky
sweet sixteen state high school tournament

between sessions we played pick up games
street ball in freedom hall we were following
the lightning quick caneyville grayson county
club they made it to the quarter final round

before going down and while i'm searching
through old photos i come across ticket stubs
and game programs and oh my there's
butch beard and oh yes wes unseld

in 1964 i was on the freshman team
centertown school when we played
breckinridge county in hardinsburg
alfred "butch" beard jr. was a junior

i'd never seen anyone jump up and touch
the top of the backboard and beard's team
was state tournament runner up that year
to senior westley sissel "wes" unseld's

louisville seneca team memorial coliseum
lexington kentucky seneca won state
in '63 and '64 but in 1965 beard brought
the bearcats to freedom hall where

they won it all butch beard was named
kentucky's mr. basketball adolf rupp wanted
him to play for the university of kentucky
and be the 1st black player in the ess-e-cee

and it looked like beard would go but in
the 11th hour he chose bernard "peck" hickman's
university of louisville where he starred
with unseld my brother brad and i

met peck hickman a gentleman from
central city we sat behind his bench
at freedom hall and watched 2 kentucky stars
play the game like it had never been played
they changed the face of college basketball
butch beard and wes unseld

sweet sixteen runner up

in the spring of 1964 for my 8th grade graduation
centertown school 300 students grades 1 through 12
i wrote and presented a speech on sportsmanship
i've always given my all every situation i find myself in
is an opportunity to grow and central to growth
is learning how to win how to lose
with dignity with integrity always respecting the person
on the other side we're all winners and losers
we all play on the same team

in the spring of 1968 age 17 i graduated
from ohio county high school highway 231
between beaver dam and hartford
1,200 students grades 9 through 12
i left home a wanderer a seeker
yearning to find to know myself
i hit the road running
excited to be on my own

in the spring of 1969 ucla defeated purdue 92 to 72
for the ncaa basketball championship
freedom hall louisville kentucky

far back as i remember i've loved music
every kind of music the more electric lightning
spirit energy the better i like it
being born a seeker a traveler i've always wanted
to stare deep into the eyes of god
since i was a boy i recognized that the love
inherent in the poetry of music in the music of poetry
is the bestest fastest way to touch god's face
to drink god's tears yes give me lightning
lightning is the closest we can come to know
god in nature i love lightning and thunder
both of which i continually discover in
the music of poetry in the poetry of music

in the spring of 1969 i was already way deep
into the poemed music of the hippie movement
i was exploring altered states of consciousness
expanding traveling seeking searching for myself
yes i was tuned in i was turned on and being
a kentucky nature boy no matter where i've traveled
no matter what i've done i've always been an athlete
i love the great outdoors i love sports and being
kentucky born basketball the commonwealth's
unofficial official religion basketball always has been

still is and always will be my favorite sport

in the spring of 1969 being born a traveler searcher
seeker i had hitchhiked to florida made it to jacksonville beach
then beautiful saint augustine when late on a wednesday
night i called home to check on my brother brad's
ohio county eagles' basketball team i knew they'd
won the 3rd region championship by defeating greenville
thus making their way into the kentucky state high school
basketball sweet sixteen tournament freedom hall
louisville kentucky but they weren't a big team shorter
than rupp's runts the tallest player was 6 feet 2 inches
so i'm sure i wasn't the only one who was skeptical
as to whether they'd make it past their 1st game but
lo and behold when i called our farmhouse home from
a jacksonville beach pay phone late on a chilly
wednesday night and mama was excited yelling
they won they won they blew away bardstown
i hitchhiked to the jacksonville airport and for the
1st time in my life boarded an airplane and flew
to standiford field louisville kentucky so yes i was
there in freedom hall friday night to scream and yell
with all the other ohio countians plus a growing
number of folks rooting for the lightning fast
passers the sharp shooters the underdog eagles
as my brother brad's team whipped louisville's
saint xavier and yes i was there for the saturday
morning semi-final overtime win over ashland
and i was there for the saturday night championship
to watch louisville's central high school handily
defeat ohio county 101 to 72 central's ron king
and otto petty went on to florida state coached
by louisvillian hugh durham they beat
the university of kentucky in the ncaa tournament
adolf rupp's last game but they were runner up
to bill walton and ucla in the championship game
so my brother brad and the ohio county eagles
held their heads high they had gone further
than anyone dreamed they could or would
they played valiantly against a gifted opponent
they learned that every situation provides
an opportunity to grow and central to growth
is learning how to win and to lose
with dignity with integrity always respecting
the person on the other side
we're all winners and losers
we all play on the same team

breaking and entering basketball

i broke into my first gym
when i was 9 years old

through my boyhood my teen years
and into my 20s i played
breaking and entering basketball

between dribbles i listened
for the sound of a principal's
a teacher's a janitor's a policeman's
footsteps in the hall

when i was 12 i wrote a letter
to the governor of kentucky
explaining the community benefits
of keeping school gyms open
at night and on weekends
anytime there weren't school
activities the governor wrote back
saying he agreed but nothing changed

so i kept playing
breaking and entering basketball

gary "lefty" raymond passed the ball to himself

late one friday night in front of the dairy freeze
in beaver dam kentucky i watched lowell tarrants

throw blinding fast punches and beat the crap
out of a young punk who had bad mouthed him

the next day i watched lowell perform an acrobatic
360 spin around his man and lay the ball off

the backboard on the opposite side with his left hand
lowell tarrants was the best allround athlete

to ever come out of ohio county he was
quarterback catcher guard and one helluva fighter

my brother brad's bicycle had v shaped handlebars
and a banana seat i had a 10 speed many times

we biked the 6 miles from our farm outside centertown
to mchenry where we played hard nosed basketball

for hours with phillip and gary "lefty" raymond their sister
alicia was a cheerleader for the centertown demons

she was a year older than me we were boyfriend
girlfriend for a little while i'll never forget the night

we rode the school bus to central city where
the centertown demons took on the golden tide

ralph mayes who went on to star at vanderbilt
played for central city while barry barnes

danny decker shelby burden doug porter
and gerald powers started for centertown

wow everyone was sweating in the standing room only
packed house central city gym it was a barn burner

we stopped for hamburgers and onion rings after
the game smoochers rode in the back of the bus

gary "lefty" raymond was the best basketball player
to ever come out of ohio county i'd never seen

anyone pass the ball to the backboard slip
around his man catch the ball and hit the layup

all in one quick fluid motion sometimes lefty
got a rebound then launched the ball downcourt

took off passing everyone caught his own pass
and made a layup the refs didn't call him for walking

cause they'd never seen anything like it before
neither had i neither had anyone else lefty led

the ohio county eagles to runner-up in the
1969 sweet sixteen kentucky state high school

basketball tournament at freedom hall in louisville
my brother brad played on that team

western kentucky university coach jim richards
gave lefty a full scholarship which he finally lost

cause well i think he lost it cause he broke so
many noses of guys who weren't fast enough

to catch his lightning passes to this day i've never
seen another basketball player come out of

ohio county western kentucky as good as
gary "lefty" raymond who passed the ball to himself

nose to nose with john danks oldham park beaver dam basketball

i deflected john's shot but he got the rebound
then i stole the ball from him and zipped

a bullet pass upcourt to brad who kissed
the backboard with an 8 foot jumper

john said ronnie you're better than
i thought i laughed it was a hard fought game

but my brother brad and tommy james
and i won i don't remember our other

2 players it was a pickup game
winner keeps playing us boys ran some

kickass streetball games in oldham park
next to the softball field beaver dam kentucky

at 85 mr. danks a fine southern gentleman
still runs the danks funeral home

i always liked the danks kids
jeff and debbie and john good folks

john played basketball 4 years at the university of texas
both his sons now play baseball for the chicago white sox

i loved growing up on a farm in western kentucky
with farms and small towns for miles all around

matanzas centertown rockport mchenry beaver dam
cromwell hartford dundee fordsville mount pleasant

no matter where i go and i go i always take
wonderful memories with me memories of playing

basketball with hard nosed good people
folks i'll forever call friends

i'll break your leg

a long time ago in a land far away
i rolled 6,000 putty balls and pushed them in

3 little holes in each of the 2,000 refrigerators
that flew by me yes i spent that summer

working 2nd shift on the whirlpool refrigerator assembly line
in evansville indiana you see i'd fallen in love

for the 1st time one night at a lake venus dance
in muhlenburg county the young woman lived on newburg road

so when i got off shift at midnight i stopped to visit
then i'd spend the night in daddy's old white chevy station wagon

down on the ohio river in the mornings i bathed
and brushed my teeth in the river

she went to western kentucky university so
i switched schools to join her but i failed all

my college classes that year cause i never
went to class i only studied sex101 but

that's another story i don't care to tell because
one day i discovered her kissing another man

the story i've come to tell is connected though you see
my friend gene williams called me in evansville on the phone

and said hey ron whatever you do you've got to go through
the lambda chi alpha ritual and i said lambda what you know

i'm not a fan of fraternities and sororities he said now look
you've got to listen to the lyrics of steppenwolf's

magic carpet ride lead singer john kay was a lambda chi
and the song is about the ritual i said okay

so i broke up with my woman who i'd found cheating on me
and i went back to georgetown college and joined a fraternity

good lord help me i wasn't a fan of fraternities but this one
was different it was filled with artists writers athletes intellectuals

and well now rebel me when the lambda chi old timers
lined us pledges up late one night and began to haze i said

hell no boys who'll walk out with me i'll not stand for hazing
so several of my pledge brothers walked out with me

i waged a war to end hazing i divided the fraternity
but guess what we won i'm still proud today of our victory

but the story i came to share my friends is about basketball
you see i played guard on the lambda chi alpha intramural team

i was reading 3 books a day drinking and doing drugs
seeing many lady friends trying to get over the pain of breaking up

from the 1st time i fell in love one day i fell out of my seat in
dr. greg's philosophy class i'd drank 6 little kings and took a hit

of mescaline i was reading all the works by and about
edmund husserl and henri bergson i was fascinated by

phenomenology and the relative nature of my existence
so on saturday morning after a night of debauchery the lambda chi's

were playing the faculty and staff team in the georgetown college gym
jake reid said if you foul me like that again i'll break your leg

jake reid played ball at ohio county high school he was from
beaver dam he was a star there and at georgetown

a fierce competitor on the court and so was i but off the court
you couldn't find a nicer guy so when jake reid said what he did

i looked him square in the eyes then laughed real loud and fouled him again
this time harder than before the game was brutal and bloody

the lambda chi's barely pulled out the win and as my story closes
i want to add a word about my friend from beaver dam

jake reid went on to coach the georgetown college tigers
basketball team for 23 seasons he led them to 529 victories

he was naia coach of the year and inducted into
the hall of fame he loved his cigarettes he died age 48

and i can still hear jake reid say
if you foul me like that again i'll break your leg

when kenny davis elbowed me i saw stars

in 1968 i was a 17 year old freshman
at georgetown college living on the 3rd floor

of anderson hall where nearly all the athletes
lived after a while i became friends with

a wild assortment of folks from all walks
of life i love sports especially basketball so

i'll never forget the pickup game
when kenny davis elbowed me i saw stars

kenny was a good guy a real character
i liked him but that night in the school gym

we were guarding each other kenny had
the ball his back to me dribbling with his

right hand i was staying low sticking too
close kenny and i played rough kenny made

a lightning move to the left then in less than
an instant he simultaneously switched the ball

to his left hand pivoting to his right elbowing me
in the chin as he flew around me to the basket

i don't recall whether kenny hit the shot or not i
reckon he did you see kenny davis georgetown college

class of 1971 scored a 4 year total of 3,003 points
setting a career record for kentucky colleges

3 times he was naia all-american and in 1972
he was captain of the usa olympic basketball team

i've had many broken bones and i have scars on
scars from playing ball and too many fights and

i've experienced numerous altered states of
consciousness but nothing quite like

when kenny davis elbowed me and i saw stars

not without a fight

nobody kicked me out of a gym
i'd broken into without a fight

i had been breaking and entering gyms
since i was a kid so i already knew

the drill but in the late 1960s at
georgetown college i became a master

you see i was not only a member of
the sds students for a democratic society

yes we led the free speech and
other movements across the country

but at georgetown with friends gene williams
and danny matherly and dale daley

i formed a clandestine group called dcm
dedicated and concerned muckrakers

danny taught me how to pick locks and
tap phones we took over campus i learned

years later that the board of directors nearly
closed the school cause of our activities

we took over the school newspaper and
student government then shut them both down

we broke into the president's office and
blocked it so no one could get in while

we broadcast rock music over loudspeakers
that sounded all over town but oh no that

wasn't all well being an athlete loving basketball
one night i broke into the gym which soon

filled with friends and strangers all students
running full court but when we heard the police

sirens most of the players ran not me i
waited you see i believed that gym should

be open to students when the school teams
weren't using it but legendary georgetown college

coach bob davis didn't see it that way he felt
the gym was his so when he and the police

stormed in yelling who broke into my gym i
said i did it's not your gym this is the school's

gym and us students have the right to play here
when you and your team aren't using it well

friends my words didn't exactly appeal to
coach davis who was almost as hard nosed

as my dad coach davis was king on campus he
was used to having his way he got in my face

and i got in his we went nose to nose he
said i'll have you arrested i said for playing

basketball he said yes get out now i said i'm not leaving
but soon i realized that i really didn't want to

spend the night in jail for playing basketball
so i turned and with the police and coach davis

staring holes through me i walked away i
met coach davis years later long after

he retired he had been inducted into the hall of fame
and was chair of the usa olympic basketball committee

he's actually a good guy and well by god so am i
we shook hands and laughed recalling that night when

nobody kicked me out of a gym
i'd broken into without a fight

104 degrees in the shade of a saguaro cactus

104 degrees in the shade
of a saguaro cactus

and us kentucky boys
my brother brad and me

we be runnin and gunnin
behind the back between the legs

but nothin too fancy simply
fast paced pass and shoot

hardnosed blue collar defense
ain't no i in team no trash talkin

grill it then drill it basketball
phoenix arizona at 6'1"

i'm guardin the 7 foot center
my brother brad at 5'10"

is guardin the 6'8" forward
best games runnin

in phoenix arizona where i live
my brother brad come to pay me a visit

october 1974 we climb squaw peak
every day oak creek canyon

not far away we wander backroads
white mountains salt river devil's curve

grand canyon gila monsters tarantulas
rattlesnakes jackalopes mile high

sand storms beers by the pool at midnight
concerts david bowie lou reed electric light orchestra

bestest hottest homemade mexican food
i've ever tasted so hot my eyeballs sweat

and basketball yep we be runnin at sundown
full court street ball damn good games and

my brother and me we be bringin it fast passin
sharp shootin now you see it now you don't

104 degrees in the shade
of a saguaro cactus

oxford ball

while punting on the cherwell near magdalen bridge
at oxford the oldest university in the english speaking world

do they play basketball here at oxford?
bill bradley played for the oxford blues 1965-67
bill clinton played for the oxford twos 1968

while taking vows swearing oaths at
the bodleian library while having sherry
with the chancellor at rhodes house

while wandering brasenose lane to
j.r.r. tolkien's exeter college where
i stayed i wondered where's the gym?

after my 1st pick up game with oxford blues
i was asked where are you from?
i replied kentucky oh rupp they said

no wonder then after 2 hours of playing
my 1st games of oxford ball
on the way out of the gym i read the sign

what is basketball?
basketball is played by two teams
made up of five players and seven
substitutes the aim of the game
for each team is to get the ball
into the elevated baskets at either
end of the court more times than
the opposition while preventing
the opposition from scoring at the
same time a game is made up of
four periods each lasting 10 minutes
of actual playing time if the scores
are tied at the end of the game
extra five-minute overtime periods
are played until a winner is declared

drenched in sweat i walked
to the eagle and child on st. giles
where tolkien and lewis shared
their new writings out loud and while
drinking amontillado medium dry sherry doubles
i read ihab hassan's the dismemberment
of orpheus toward a postmodern literature

and i played
oxford ball

elbow at the y

some of the best former
high school and college and pro players
on the planet but don't ever
forget the street ballers
many as good and some better than
the x and o ers

elbow at the y
kentucky outlaw basketball
poetry in motion
the greatest show on earth

4 minutes to go tie game
fighting for the championship
lexington kentucky ymca winter league
i'm shooting 66% for the season
yes i keep stats in my head
keep the score for every game out loud
been doing it since i was a kid
so i'm red hot shootin the lights out
when the other team sends in their thug sub
who replaces my man 1st play
he turns and with all his might
intentionally elbows me in the mouth
knocks out a front tooth the ref stops
the game i spit tooth fragments splinters
and blood the ref throws out the thug
and asks if i'm alright i say let's play
we win the game by a basket

elbow at the y
kentucky outlaw basketball
poetry in motion
the greatest show on earth

sucker punched at freedom hall basketball

spring 1996 freedom hall 3 on 3 street ball jamboree
games for all ages coaching my son Dylan's team
in the 13 and 14 years old age group

we won our 10am game by a basket
against a damn good team that included
a 6 foot 8 inch player who went on
to star for the university of louisville
where i'm a professor

our 1pm game is a street brawl
filled with arguments and name calling
and hard intentional fouls

the other team's parents are worse
than their kids yelling obscenities
at our players and me but we ignore them
which makes them worse

we lose by a basket my kids are upset
they run off the court i always teach
and practice tough play but good
sportsmanship so i turned to my right
to get my boys and have them
shake hands with the other team

but when i turn a big muscular guy
weighing at least 50 pounds more
than my 160 pound wiry thin frame
is blowing his bad breath into my face
he's backed up by all the other team's
parents the bully says are you staring
at her in a flash i glance at the women
to see if one is worth staring at then
i look back to bully and grinning say no
he says are you laughing at me

i realize now that even though his team
won he wants to fight to show off his macho
man abilities so i turn yet again to go
find my boys but the next thing i know
i'm on the floor with everything spinning
i touch my face it's bashed in badly broken
in many places i lift my arm searching for
someone to help me up the bully is running
with one of our mothers chasing him through
freedom hall yelling stop him he hit our coach

finally the court monitor sees me and comes
over i say please get the police and an
ambulance my cheek is sunk in my jaw is
moved over my nose is turned toward my
cheek i'm finally taken to the hospital

he must have had brass knuckles i've
received many blows to the face via sports
and fights but never anything this bad

i end up having 2 surgeries to straighten
my face i have a broken nose broken cheek
broken and permanently dislocated jaw
and a concussion

i wear braces and wires for 3 years when
i teach and give readings and recordings
i split blood onto the page wires cutting
the inside of my mouth but i don't let
any of it slow me down i kept teaching
with douglas brinkley i produced the
48 hour non-stop music and poetry
new orleans insomniacathon 1996 at
the new orleans contemporary art center
the mermaid lounge and the howlin wolf club
in december 1996 i produced the official
hunter s. thompson tribute with hunter and
his mom virginia and his son juan and
johnny depp and warren zevon and roxanne
pulitzer and david amram and doug brinkley
and i recorded a new cd and wrote a new book
and produced many events and published
many titles and did a performance tour
of the netherlands and continued raising
three children and when i had a half hour break
i rested in the dark to help the migraines subside

the bully got one year community service he
chose to serve it by spending half a day each
week at a local catholic girls' high school plus
he paid some of my medical expenses
i got stuck having to pay over 10 grand myself
my dad and my brother wanted the bully's name
they were ready to give him the gift of kentucky
backwoods justice and i wanted that to happen
i had revenge nightmares for years it was a
spiritual crisis for me i thanked my family but
told them i had to handle the situation on my own

karma the law of cause and effect for every action
there's an equal and opposite reaction

so i started working harder on myself to heal
the rage within and i'm happy to say
that though i still have plenty of rage
great healing has taken place

since i was sucker punched
at freedom hall

from kentucky to alphabet city

runnin and gunnin the puerto ricans and me
street ball chain nets shirts and skins from kentucky to alphabet city

thompson square park lower east side new york city
august 2nd 1997 i called john giorno but was told

he'd flown to lawrence kansas where william s. burroughs is dying
between games i say a prayer while drinking water from the fountain

i pray for allen ginsberg who crossed over in april
and i pray for old bull lee

after the games shake hands say see you on down the road
then i wander over to visit my friend the blind poet saint

of the lower east side steve cannon
a gathering of the tribes

there's an elderly gentleman who sits on the stoop
outside steve's walkup he's there every time

i visit we pick up our conversation where it left off
as if it never ended friends from another lifetime

oh friendship never ends friendship never ends
well it's finally showtime so i wander up to

the nuyorican poets cafe so many magical shows
a big hug for miguel algorin

the place is packed tonight standing room only
a young puerto rican spoken word hip hop crowd

with the david amram trio i read mama and sex education
then at the last minute i change my set list and

perform calling the toads a poem i wrote for burroughs
at sunrise i picked up a new york times and read

that william s. burroughs died at the same time
i was reading at the nuyorican poets cafe lower east side

oh friendship never ends friendship never ends
thompson square park lower east side new york city

runnin and gunnin the puerto ricans and me
street ball chain nets shirts and skins from kentucky to alphabet city

Watching the NBA playoffs with Hunter S. Thompson

Hunter shot himself. He is gone.
He died in his kitchen in his cabin at
Owl Farm Woody Creek Colorado.

I read his Nixon obituary,
"He Was A Crook,"
which I published
in the Published in Heaven Poster Series,
and other works to him in that kitchen.

I took my children to visit him.
He loved young people. He loved his family.

I drank and did drugs with him.
We watched basketball.

One night, years ago, in early May
my son Nathanial and I arrived,
driving 24 hours non-stop from Kentucky,
just in time to watch the NBA playoffs with Hunter.
Don Johnson called several times
wanting us to come over.

Kentuckian Rex Chapman
was playing for the Phoenix Suns.
The Suns were down by nine points
with one minute to go in the game.
I looked at Hunter and said
I'll bet you
that Rex will hit three threes
and tie the game,
that the Suns will win
by one point in three overtimes.

Hunter looked at me and laughed.
Rex hit three threes
and tied the game.
But Phoenix lost
in three overtimes,
by one point.
I got damn close.
Hunter paid closer attention to me after that.
We talked about life
about our families about literature.
Hunter was a good kind man.
He was full of life.
He was tough.
He was a real human being.
He was spirit, holy spirit,
no matter what anyone says.

the comeback kid

i'm 65 years old now
and basketball remains
my forever favorite sport

i stride into the gym
at the ymca

10 black cats
in their early 20s
are running 5 on 5
full court

2 white cats
in their early 20s
are standing at the end
of the court

i walk up and say
"you got next?"
the bigger white cat says
"you ever play?"

i get right up in his face
and give him my meanest
i'll break both your legs look
and snarling say

"why don't you find out!"
he takes one step back
and squeaks "ok"
so we pick up

2 players from
the losing team
for the next
hour and a half

we win every game
then i tell my team
i have to leave
i've got a poetry reading to give

one of them says
"what's your story?"
i promise to share it
another day but i add

i'm making a comeback
from a series
of near death experiences
plus i quit drinking

3 years ago
and now at 65 years of age
i'm getting younger and older
faster than ever

i've never felt my age
they stare wide eyed amazed
so now whenever
i stride into the gym

at the ymca
the black cats and the white cats
in their early 20s
they yell and wave

and pick me to play
on their team
they call me
the comeback kid

www.ingramcontent.com/pod-product-compliance
Lightning Source LLC
LaVergne TN
LVHW041551070426
835507LV00011B/1031